Responses to
Derek Jarman's *Blue* (1993)

Pilot Press
London

Screen Two

I was to welcome you and accompany you to your seat in Screen Two. A wheelchair had been arranged, a space reserved in the auditorium.

Someone dropped you off at reception. It wasn't Keith.
He arrived after the film had started.

Your suit dressed a body ravaged by illness and prescription drugs. Your glasses obscured eyes that couldn't see. Yet, this radiating presence. A seductive energy.

The screening was about to begin. 'No need for the wheelchair', you said, 'we'll walk'.

I guided you into the cinema towards your seat, your hand resting on my arm, our bodies linked like dancing partners.

Warm applause.
Animated voices.

The lights went out.
The screen turned blue.

I lost myself in blue,
saw and heard only blue.

'Blue is darkness made visible.'

Roelof Bakker

Impatient youths of the sun: death, psychedelia and the creative kinship between Derek Jarman and Coil

A little over halfway through *Blue*, Derek Jarman talks of drugs. Not the kind that allows one to trip, to transgress the fragile body, but rather the kind that keeps his body — deteriorating with autoimmune disease — from dying.

The nurse explains the implant
You mix the drugs and drip yourself once a day
The drugs are kept in a small fridge they give you

Jarman's body is heavy baggage in the airport of his mind, journeying back through memories of past indiscretions, of present-oriented *jouissance* that preceded the finality of here and now.

Can you imagine traveling around with that? The metal implant will set the bomb detector off at airports
And I could just see myself traveling to Berlin with a fridge under my arm

In a whisk of reverb, airport muzak blurs into the rhythmic tremolo effects of a psychedelic disco track.

Impatient youths of the sun
Burning with many colours
Flick combs through hair in bathroom mirrors

This could be the most vivid and hallucinatory moment of Jarman's *Blue*, largely for the palpable oddity of the warped dancefloor music soundtracking the scene.

Fucking with fusion and fashion
Dance in the beams of emerald lasers

For a minute, a string section more typical of gay discos of the 1970s and early '80s begins, whisking listeners into an orgasmic moment of familiar ecstasy — bringing to mind sex, a huff of poppers, or a come up on MDMA.

Mating on suburban duvets
Cum-splattered nuclear breeders

Just as soon as this climactic instrumentation arrives, it abruptly morphs into a dissonant and unsettling drone.

What a time that was.

The musical score driving this narrative was produced by Coil, a group of experimental musicians consisting primarily of partners John Balance and Peter "Sleazy" Christopherson, with other regular collaborators such as in this particular instance Danny Hyde. Founded in 1983, Coil emerged from a distinctive London avant garde scene that notably included the band Psychic TV, in which Christopherson and Balance were for a time members. The duo became friends with Jarman through this community, with Coil providing music for his feature *The Angelic Conversation* in 1985. There was something of a kindred spirit between these artists. Both Jarman and Coil dealt with their anachronistic subject matter by applying a dark sense of camp, one that in a way managed to unpick something weird and rotten at the heart of Englishness. They were uniquely strange but together not strange bedfellows. However their artistic paths coalesced best in *Blue*.

Coil's music was consistently concerned with themes of sexuality, death and psychedelia. In the sense that the term psychedelic means etymologically to 'manifest' the 'mind,' this concept — as demonstrated in the work of Coil — holds a particular weight in the gay world. From the hallucinatory films of Kenneth Anger, to the trippy disco of Patrick Cowley, to the drug fuelled euphoria and addiction of chemsex, psychedelia can be regarded as a persistent tenet in queer cultures hyperaware of the body's tender transcience.

Gays know of escaping or challenging their bodies. Queer theory has for decades been concerned with a tendency towards self-annihilation, the death drive and *jouissance* in gay male culture, both arguing for and against this identification. How much of this is from homophobic institutions pathologising gay men? How much is it a grave of their own ecstatic making? As Guy Hocquenghem wrote in 1972, a decade before the discovery of AIDS, but preempting the painful dismissal of the disease as one self-inflicted by delinquent gays and junkies: "drugs and homosexuality are generally mentioned together in official reports because they seem to hold similar positions in the process of degeneration."

Coil were no stranger to these themes, nor to stimulants, and they embraced the psychedelic as an aesthetic and conceptual foundation, releasing recordings that were described as "music to take drugs by" by Balance himself. But also, the group developed their early work around confronting, and moving past, the bounds of the dying body. In the mid-1980s, Balance and Christopherson's friends started to fall ill to a plague, misleadingly dubbed then "Gay-Related Immune Deficiency". They produced two remarkable albums exploring death in direct response to this trauma, 1984's *Scatology* and *Horse Rotorvator* in 1986.

By 1994, the plague had taken yet another of their friends. *Blue* is a very psychedelic film, and as Jarman's bodily deterioration led him to manifest sonic visions of his mind and memories of his life, Coil were perfect collaborators for this melding of death, sexuality and bodily transgression. One might say that Jarman's work was in fact always psychedelic, however with a certain postmodern self-awareness. His films referenced the Englishness which abounded in the flower power of the 1960s and its folk revival, though with no small serving of irony. Jarman's aesthetic, like Coil's, was one of a more queered and dark psychedelia. *Blue* is not just a eulogy to a life lived well, but a swansong to this unique creative kinship between three friends and collaborators — John, Peter and Derek — who knew a thing or two about tripping through queerness and death.

In 1994 Coil released a commemorative 7" record with unique versions of their brief track that appeared in Jarman's final film, pressing 1000 blue vinyls, and 23 yellow (perhaps, if I were to guess, a reference to Jarman's 23 years of filmmaking). Writing in their newsletter to fans, under the poignant heading "The Last of England" — not many saw Englishness in quite the same way that Jarman did — Coil wrote of the filmmaker's funeral:

"Derek's body, dressed in a robe of gold[,] was lying in state when we arrived at the little wooden house on the beach that had been his home for the last years of his life. He looked fabulous - like some kind of lovingly sculpted wax figure."

Jared Davis

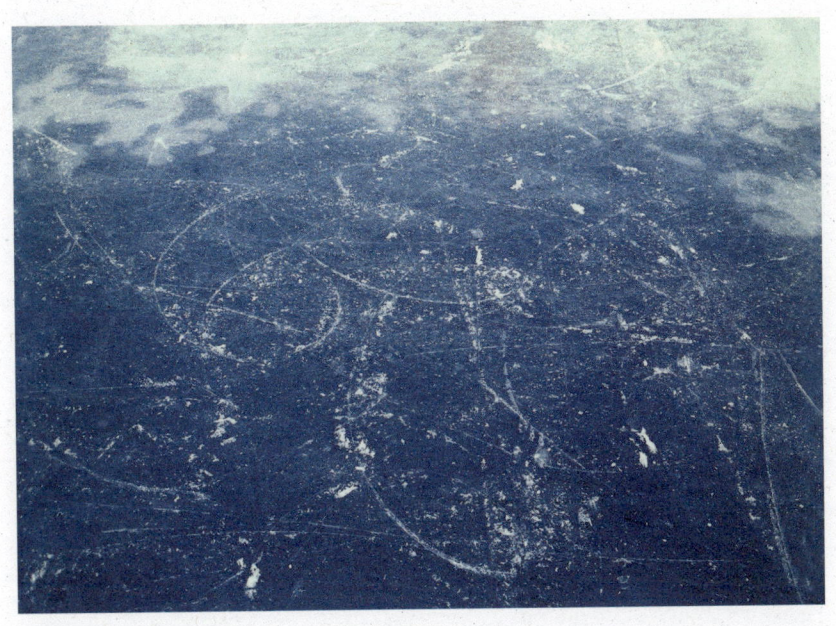

Becca Albee

these were thy merchants (loops of blue)

& blue,
moreover thou shalt make the tabernacle with ten curtains of fine twined
                                                                       linen, & blue,
& thou shalt make loops of blue
& thou shalt make a vail of blue,
& thou shalt make a hanging for the door of the tent, of blue,
& for the gate of the court shall be a hanging of twenty cubits, of blue,
& they shall take gold, & blue,
& they shall make the ephod of gold, of blue,
& the curious girdle of the ephod, which is upon it, shall be of the same,
                         according to the work thereof; even of gold, of blue,
& thou shalt make the breastplate of judgment with cunning work; after
                         the work of the ephod thou shalt make it; of gold, of blue,
& they shall bind the breastplate by the rings thereof unto the rings of the
                                      ephod with a lace of blue,
& thou shalt make the robe of the ephod all of blue.
& beneath upon the hem of it thou shalt make pomegranates of blue,
& thou shalt put it on a blue
& blue,
& every man, with whom was found blue,

& all the women that were wise hearted did spin with their hands, &
                         brought that which they had spun, both of blue,

    them hath he filled with wisdom of heart, to work all manner of work, of
            the engraver, & of the cunning workman, & of the embroiderer,
                                            in blue,
    & every wise hearted man among them that wrought the work of the
                tabernacle made ten curtains of fine twined linen, & blue,
    & he made loops of blue
    & he made a vail of blue,
    & he made a hanging for the tabernacle door of blue,
    & the hanging for the gate of the court was needlework, of blue,
    & with him was _____, son of _____, of the tribe of ___, an
            engraver, & a cunning workman, & an embroiderer in blue,
    & of the blue,
    & he made the ephod of gold, blue,
    & they did beat the gold into thin plates, & cut it into wires, to work it in
                                                        the blue
    & the curious girdle of his ephod, that was upon it, was of the same,
                      according to the work thereof; of gold, blue,
    & he made the breastplate of cunning work, like the work of the ephod;
                                                      of gold, blue,
    & they did bind the breastplate by his rings unto the rings of the ephod
                                                      with a lace of blue,
    & he made the robe of the ephod of woven work, all of blue.

    & they made upon the hems of the robe pomegranates of blue,
    & a girdle of fine twined linen, & blue

& they tied unto it a lace of blue,
& shall put thereon the covering of badgers' skins, & shall spread over it a
cloth wholly of blue,
& upon the table of shewbread they shall spread a cloth of blue,
& they shall take a cloth of blue,
& upon the golden altar they shall spread a cloth of blue,
& they shall take all the instruments of ministry, wherewith they minister
in the sanctuary, & put them in a cloth of blue,
speak unto the children of _____, & bid them that they make them
fringes in the borders of their garments throughout their
generations, & that they put upon the fringe of the borders a
ribband of blue:
send me now therefore a man cunning to work in gold, & in silver, & in
brass, & in iron, & in purple, & crimson, & blue,
the son of a woman of the daughters of ___, & his father was a man of
____, skilful to work in gold, & in silver, in brass, in iron, in
stone, & in timber, in purple, in blue,
& he made the vail of blue,
where were white, green, & blue,
hangings, fastened with cords of fine linen & purple to silver rings &
pillars of marble: the beds were of gold & silver, upon a
pavement of red, & blue,

& _____ went out from the presence of the king in royal apparel of
blue

the blue
silver spread into plates is brought from _____, & gold from _____,
        the work of the workman, & of the hands of the founder: blue
which were clothed with blue,
fine linen with broidered work from _____ was that which thou spreadest
                                          forth to be thy sail; blue
these were thy merchants in all sorts of things, in blue

Linda Kemp

Remembering ahead

Language kneads the room into velvet,
my mouth a quiet catacomb and outside
the snowflakes are bigger today. Dreams
of reversing trucks, a wild daughter
on the wing, beard rethinking itself, farm
scratches, pie nights. Our window
withdraws into the street. Crowded by
visions you fall sky to sea to sky,
With coughing hips, pelvis articulates a love,
a twirl of cotton candy in a bowl, a key
whispers a name at dawn and you open.
Blue prism in the red blood, the wall sighs.
I promise not to ask how you died, the premise
of love. I kiss you and kiss you again. I'm left
behind, our love, quiet as a clue.

Ashleigh A. Allen

Magpie

Some creatures value the human, take
a shine to the colour blue, for example, even though blue
things neither nourish or preserve them; even so, make

blue their life's work and seek blue out,
build keepsake
shrines from scraps of denim, spearmint
wrappers, For You From Corfu
tat, the marzipan balloons
on a gender reveal cake;

some creatures mean *boy*, some more mean *girl*;
some mean *earthquake*
when seen on higher ground, which means
they have abandoned you;
some hold funerals for their dead,
some undertake

to divvy up the dead one's blue things;
some would call you snowflake
if you flinched at this, since some are so inured to death
that death is déjà vu;
some know ritual for bullshit, but perform it anyway,
for performance sake;

some consume as performance: whatever bread there is
to break, they break,
no matter if it's steak or carrion, songless bug or songbird –
nothing's off the menu
for some creatures; some creatures would sooner bite the hand
than bear the handshake;

some themselves are blue; they might not break
this news until they're seen in flight, a sky-tattoo;
some creatures, like tattoos, are a mistake.
Take the magpie for example. Take it.

David Nash

untitled (an epic in fragments)

The chorus sing of *lesbian boys*, of *psycho fags* and an unseen monster, the *Hetero demon*. They are cut through, in two, by the propulsive power of a military chant. One man calls: *I am a gay.* His comrades in arms respond: HE IS A GAY.

The soldiers are kissed by the sun, wishing their lips could take the place of one of its luminous rays, afraid of what it would illuminate in them. They are somewhere between agony and ecstasy, between the silent pain of stoicism, and the terrifying, liberating un known of confession.

The war rages across the news papers as much as it does the front lines. **The soldiers** are captured behind enemy headlines. Not a soul wants to fight, but no man can lay down his arms. If they did, they'd be defence less. Worse than being naked.

The boy sees things differently. A prophet who talked to and through the camera in the 50s and 60s might call it a *purple testament,* but **the boy** calls it, and him self, Blue.

The boy can see that the world is coming to an
end, that **the soldiers** in his battalion are
racing towards it even as they *rage against the
dying of the light*, all those bright colours that
fade to black.

The soldiers are taken on a journey by **the
ferryman**, a shepherd for the lost. His world is
quiet, and **the war** is muffled, heard from another
room. Here **the soldiers** stand on an
indigo shore, brought by boat across a
cobalt sea, studying above them for the hint of a change in a
jet black sky.

The boy hopes that he knows where they're
going, that their final destination is the same as a
place he saw once; in a memory or a
dream. From before **the war**, and before the world was
Blue. Once upon a time, he heard **the chorus** sing of
what it was like to dance in-between
emerald green lasers. **The boy** thinks the lasers were shooting
up from the floor. That outside, there was a sign on the
door, and it might have said
HEAVEN. **The boy** hopes that he knows where they're going.

Sam Moore

You are not alone

March 4, 2019: I groggily wake up in San Francisco to a headline in the *New York Times* online that reads "HIV Is Reported Cured in a Second Patient, a Milestone in the Global AIDS Epidemic."[1] I circle around the sentence a few times, trying to parse the matter-of-fact candor in which the "milestone" news is delivered, less as a declaration and more as a statement of inevitability. I read on. Initial tests, while hopeful, suggest long-term remission rather than an outright cure, while the treatment itself — a radical bone-marrow transplant primarily intended to treat leukemia in the patients observed — is dangerous, with its own set of harmful, even life-threatening, side effects.

The *Times* refers to the two men who've been "cured" as "the Berlin patient" and "the London patient," pseudonyms that evoke romantic associations with the urbane. I keep stumbling whenever I read the London patient's name, my mind drifting to sweeping cinematic melodrama, a faux nostalgia for empire, and images of Kristen Scott Thomas trapped in a cave at the edge of the desert, waiting for a rescue that never comes.

I awaken further in the morning haze, thinking about what would happen if a cure were *actually* discovered in my lifetime. Would the earth crack in two, and the proverbial heavens break? Or would the news pass by unobserved, the announcement quickly obscured by a pop-up for a two-for-one sale on sneakers? Maybe I should just be happy that *anyone* is talking about HIV, especially when so many people think of the AIDS crisis as a historical event and not as the ongoing public health emergency it is.

---

[1] Mandavilli, Apoorva. "HIV Is Reported Cured in a Second Patient, a Milestone in the Global AIDS Epidemic."
New York Times (online), March 4, 2019.

A professor in my graduate program once told me that an object or event needs time before it can become a topic of study, more precisely *thirty* years of historical "distance."

I turn thirty this year. Do I have enough distance from my past to reflect on it as an object of historical inquiry? And do we need yet another thirty years before we can talk about the possible impacts of a cure in a society believing itself to be post-crisis?

Bullshit, I say. We don't have that kind of time, not when people are still sick.

We've got five years / what a surprise[2]

I've never lived in a time without HIV/AIDS; it's always been part of my lexicon, normalized to the point that I can write about it with relative ease. But I cannot imagine a post-HIV reality, perhaps because I never knew a world before AIDS. I think of those people who lost so much during the early years of the crisis: how do they talk about it? Are they able to share their experiences? Or is it still too painful?

Language fails us when we need it most. Then again, words are just too fucking limited to express our deepest grief, the kind that seeps into our bones, and into our core.

I think it's a pain cry / and I said: pain cry? / then language is a virus[3]

The scientists who commented on the findings suggest that they have two primary objectives at this juncture: to replicate the results of these initially successful procedures and to develop an effective treatment that

---

[2] David Bowie, "Five Years," *The Rise and Fall of Ziggy Stardust and the Spiders from Mars,* RCA Records, 1972.

[3] Laurie Anderson, "Language is a Virus from Outer Space," *Language is a Virus from Outer Space,* Warner Bros. Records, 1986.

can be more widely administered before the virus adapts and evolves. The hyper-resilient cells in the transplanted bone marrow have also mutated to block infection through CCR5, a protein resting on immune cells that, in its unmutated form, allows HIV to permeate through the membrane and infect its host.

The designation CCR5 is chillingly clinical, reducing language to alphanumerical identification. I feel anxious, maybe even a little paranoid. I think to myself that our greatest fears are the ones that we cannot name, let alone comprehend — the unknowable. I can almost hear David Bowie's sinister croon from the album *Station to Station*. TVC 15. CCR5. A moniker all-too-ready for a dystopian soundtrack.

Oh, so demonic, oh, my TVC 15 / transition / transmission[4]

Mutations aren't just a means of survival; they force a cell or a body to weaponize, to become a protective force or, by equal turn, an agent of harm. Procedures like bone marrow transplants remind us that our bodies are both very simple *and* impossibly complex. It's a mental trip that seems so easy: if your bodily tissue stops functioning, just swap out sick cells for healthy ones. Choose well-being over disease a few more years over a matter of months.

And then the inevitable realities kick back in: bodies exhaust themselves, quietly failing in ways we can't perceive or understand. Yeats must've been in on it when he wrote that *things fall apart; the centre cannot hold* — a foreboding dissolution distilled into an unsettling line of verse.[5]

I'm struggling to keep it together, to find an even-keeled headspace to think about epidemic and mortality. And then I think of the people who

---

[4] David Bowie, "TVC 15," *Station to Station,* RCA Records, 1976.

[5] Yeats, W.B. "The Second Coming." Poem originally published in 1919.

don't have the option to *think* about disease as an abstract concept, but who have to live through it, every day.

I knock myself back into place as I continue to wake up.

The scientists interviewed by the *Times* suggest "rearming the body with immune cells…modified to resist HIV might well succeed as a practical treatment." It's a quiet but salient metaphor, an image of immune cells as both armor and ammunition, steeling healthy tissue from harm while attacking invasive bodies. But there's also an inherent discomfort in recognizing how readily we're able to imagine the human body and its functions through the language of war.

I think about the implications of "rearming," and its suggestion of a phantom or lost limb that can only be restored by turning the body into a weapon — by replacing it with an appendage that's ready to fight. Language reveals how readily we accept systems of power by adopting and normalizing their vernaculars. The military industrial complex is giving us a complex, and it's making us sicker by the day.

Where was that protection that I needed? / Air can hurt you, too.[6]

I head to the kitchen to make breakfast, bringing my laptop to the table. As I scroll up to re-read the article, I'm startled anew by the header image, which depicts a red and orange globule surrounded by smaller emerald-green circles, scattered around the perimeter like confetti or micro greens around an egg yolk. Arrestingly lovely, its sense of form and color immediately appeals to the visual language of formal abstraction. The caption notes that the rendering depicts "a colored transmission electron micrograph of the HIV virus, in green, attaching to a white blood cell, in orange."

---

[6] Talking Heads, "Air," *Fear of Music,* Sire Records, 1979.

My brain feels deceived — I thought white blood cells would be white — and struggles with the misrecognition. Disease apparently can take on the guise of beauty. But is the virus itself beautiful, or is it just how the image has been rendered? I remember a recent conversation with a data scientist, who explained that specific colors are often applied to visual renderings to both distinguish unique elements in a composition and make them more easily legible to viewers. We dress up hard truths, sugarcoat them, so that we can soften the blow when we break difficult news.

Still, I feel angry with the scientists who generated the image for letting their aesthetic sensibilities get the better of them. But the color choices have a purpose — to visually distinguish the virus from healthy cells. I soon realize that I'm angry with myself for finding the image beautiful, for failing to correlate the micrograph with the weight of the story below. My mind flashes to a street sign by artist Anthony Discenza that reads "PRETTY PICTURES WON'T SOLVE ANYTHING." No shit, I think to myself.

I open the refrigerator and reach for an egg and some salad greens for breakfast. As I crack the egg, I stare into the yolk, then look back at my screen at the image of the orange-tinted cell under attack. It's an uncanny visual parallel. I lose my appetite.

Nobody's permanent / Everything's on loan here[7]

March 8, 2019: I turn on my phone to read the *Times* online. The app opens a video simulation that depicts "material smashed away from an asteroid following a collision" as it is "attracted back to the object by its gravity." The asteroid is rendered as an orange-red globe, with yellow shards splintering from, and recoiling back towards, its perimeter. The formal similarities to the HIV electron micrograph are

---

[7] The Pretenders, "Time the Avenger," *Learning to Crawl*, Sire Records, 1984.

alarming; the *Times* must have a perverse fascination with blending beauty with annihilation. Then again, the visual language around depicting life-threatening forces must be limited: red and orange signals danger and volatility. Encounter at your own risk.

The accompanying article notes that astronomers and scientists are preparing for the inevitability that asteroids (not singular, but plural) will approach the earth's orbit. Detonation apparently is out of the question, since asteroids have a "resilient core" with a gravitation pull so strong that asteroids "don't just absorb mind-boggling amounts of damage, but, as previous work has hinted, they also are able to rebuild themselves."[8]

It's hard not to be impressed by the fact that asteroids not only resist human interventions and attacks, they can actually generate strength from them. That fear of the unknowable rears its head again. Knowledge may be power, but what do you do with the knowledge that there are forces out there that may be unstoppable or incurable? Weaponization is not a be-all, end-all strategy. Sometimes, fighting back is not enough.

The doctors who authored the report on the bone marrow transplants noted that the cured patients were still vulnerable to "a form of HIV called X4, which employs a different protein, CXCR4, to enter cells." The imperative here is to force the immune system to adapt and evolve as quickly as it can, before the virus learns its tricks and figures out that the rug has been pulled out from underneath it. And even that isn't sure protection against viral strains that may not have been identified yet: hope with a caveat, a sense of urgency, and no guarantees.

But it has to start somewhere.

---

[8] Andrews, Robin George. "If We Blow Up an Asteroid, It Might Put Itself Back Together." *New York Times* (online), March 8, 2019.

The light / begin to bleed / begin to breathe / begin to speak[9]

March 9, 2019: I walk into Printed Matter in New York. The cold air outside prevents my mind from spinning thoughts of viruses and impact events. It's one of the few benefits of freezing temperatures: the physical discomfort shocks you back into your body. I head over to a table of recent releases from small presses and immediately see three volumes by Pilot Press from the UK, which are identified as queer anthologies on loneliness, rage, and joy (sickness, I'm told, will be published later in the spring).

Three choices — with a compelling argument for each. I tell myself that I can get one, as if this were some test of moral fortitude. It's funny how these decisions, however arbitrary, can feel impactful in the moment. Like nearly everyone I know, rage has become a default disposition, especially as our political and economic environments become even more untenable. But it's the apathy that gets to me: the all-too-willing indifference to the vulnerability of others. That's the story of oppression in this country.

It's also the history of reportage on HIV/AIDS. Take another look at Lawrence K. Altman's article "Rare Cancer Seen in 41 Homosexuals," which ran on page A20 of the *New York Times* on July 3, 1982. Altman's report is widely considered the first report on the virus (then referred to as GRID) in a major news source. The article is also queerphobic bullshit, with remarks from a physician that "there was no apparent danger to nonhomosexuals from contagion," and that "the best evidence against contagion…is that no cases have been reported to date outside the homosexual community or in women."[10]

---

[9] Kate Bush, "The Morning Fog," *Hounds of Love*, EMI Records, 1985.

[10] Altman, Lawrence K. "Rare Cancer Seen in 41 Homosexuals." *New York Times* (print). July 3, 1982. A20.

When I think of this, I try to calm down and remember how misinformation circulated in the early years of the epidemic. But, no. The article was always meant to be a throw-away, banished to the back of the paper where it could quietly run and be forgotten. Queer people didn't matter, not to the *Times*, and not to its readers. When Altman's article went to print, it ran side-bar to a full-page reproduction of sheet music for "The Star-Spangled Banner," ready to clip out for celebrations the next day. A banner headline implores readers to *Sing out on the 4th,* and the juxtaposition feels impossibly cruel: a public-health crisis deafened by the promise of fireworks and celebration and song.

My anger surges again as I flip through the books on the table. I take a look at the next title — loneliness — and wonder if anger and loneliness aren't so far off from one another. The cautious hope of an HIV cure that might not actually be a cure certainly made me feel helpless in a way that I hadn't anticipated. That's the bite of hope, isn't it? Despondency can sneak up on you if you don't assume it blindly. And it's hard to feel joy when I think about my queer ancestors and all the people who held on to that hope that they'd be part of something bigger, who remained positive and fought back and *still* never made it.

Joy feels increasingly precarious, perhaps even irresponsible, when faced with our deeply troubled and fucked-up world. And there are many days when it's just too damn hard and painful to muster it up. But when I remember those queer ancestors, and the people who came before me, I also think about how they shaped my relationship to art and activism. Hell, I think about how they shaped my sense of self; without them, I wouldn't have the tools to figure out who I am. That's something to feel pretty fucking joyful about.

And it's my responsibility — and yours — to honor those we've lost by feeling joy and rage and loneliness. It is our responsibility to carve out livable lives for ourselves. Denying our own capacity to feel, and the capacity of others to feel — that's the killer. And we certainly need hope, for fuck's sake. Without it, what's the point?

Inside the store, I calm down and open the third anthology to find a poem by JD Scott:

> Let's maintain this brain
> where we see each other
> not as their world seeks
> to see us   making us
>   into fool's gold
>
> but as we see each other
> together   in this now
>   beaming
> inside all this inebriated joy.[11]

Let's keep seeing each other inside this inebriated joy. Repeat. Fight. Live.

Jump out of the plane / there is no pilot / you / are not / alone[12]

---

[11] Scott, J.D. "Golden Calf," in *Over there: A queer anthology of joy*. London: *Pilot Press*, 2017. Unpaginated.

[12] Laurie Anderson, "From the Air," *Big Science*, Warner Bros. Records, 1982.

Anton Stuebner

after forever

    o, blue   feeling
    traffic light of sorts,   all sorts.

    i see you in windows
    thick with freezing sugar,
                        absent one.
                        absent ones.
    it's not up to wanting,
    just wanting,   you know,
    but the impossibility to have.

    so,   let have.

    the flowers in bloom,
    the tall grass wind swept,
    just for you.
                        you,
    the days and days held hostage
    on the face of the moon.

    before the endless night is out,
    we'll know what
    makes the eye an eye,   the organ bit of seeing,
                                  the twitch in the spine.

                                the glance in the liver,
                                the blink in the rectum.

                                the you in the lip,
                                becoming lips.

Gonçalo Lamas

Blue Tomorrow

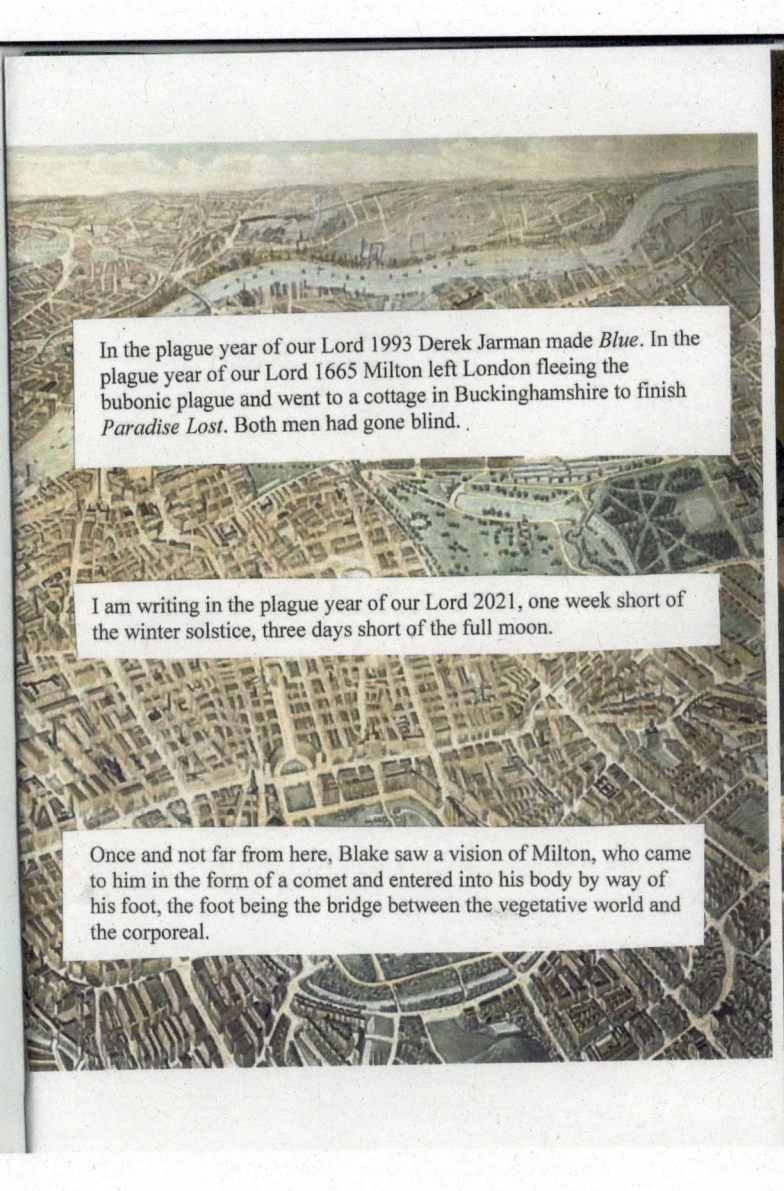

In the plague year of our Lord 1993 Derek Jarman made *Blue*. In the plague year of our Lord 1665 Milton left London fleeing the bubonic plague and went to a cottage in Buckinghamshire to finish *Paradise Lost*. Both men had gone blind.

I am writing in the plague year of our Lord 2021, one week short of the winter solstice, three days short of the full moon.

Once and not far from here, Blake saw a vision of Milton, who came to him in the form of a comet and entered into his body by way of his foot, the foot being the bridge between the vegetative world and the corporeal.

Milton came to Blake as a comet, and Jarman dreamt of Blake, in his cottage without, playing at Adam and Eve in his garden naked in Lambeth.

On waking this afternoon I calculated that my body was equidistant between that of Blake, in the dissenters' burying place of Bunhill Fields, and of Milton, who was buried at St-Giles-Without-Cripplegate.

Later, his grave was opened and desecrated.

Later still obliterated by

bombs.

The journeyman's Eden, the medieval paradise. A reliquary adorned with pearls and seaweed. A garden without walls.

The dead mount up. The dead are not equal to all the people alive on the earth. The balance is amiss. In *Paradise Lost*, God weighs the pendulous round earth on a scales, with ballanc't Aire in counterpoise.

The air then was stinking and full of the dark particles of sea coal, which blistered the lungs and brought early death.

Satan swims through the solid air of hell and the archangel Raphael praises the sweet air of Eden, so pure and fragrant it could make an angel reel.

When I woke the air was lavender and for blocks of time it grew thicker, which is to say darker, which is to say more concentrated, the colour intensifiying upon itself.

I don't like blue I once said and someone else said oh we all like blue.

Of course I do like blue

Especially just before night. Especially the sea.

Perhaps, possibly, you can't know yourself unless you are alone.

St Giles Without. Chalfont St Giles. Dungeness, where Jarman re-enacted the martyrdom of Christ, his Christ dressed in pink robes, as indeed he is in medieval paintings.

Places without the city, where possibly a comet might enter into your bloodstream by way of your foot.

What I am primarily interested in now is the creation of paradise on earth and I do not mind if it is a creation that lasts only a moment since my understanding of time has undergone a vast shift

Which is to say there is only one time: now. And the nowness of it is like the skin on a lion, like a flea on a rhinoceros. All the time, time without is swelling inside now.

Everything occurring at once, the names of the plagues spoken at once, the people rising up and speaking all together.

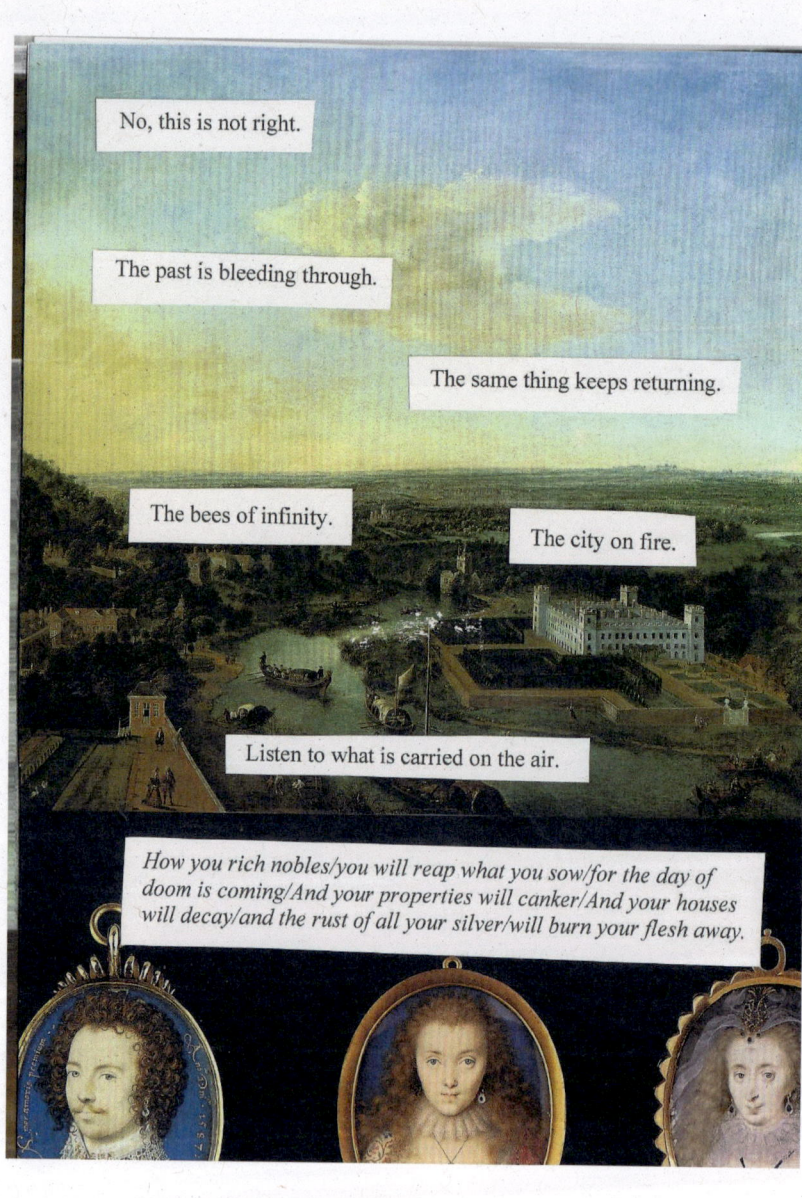

I picture Derek dancing to it, in pandemonium.

The pandemonium of images.

The club is called Heaven. It is underneath the city.

Blake dancing, a comet in his foot.

I won't be dancing.

I came here to watch.

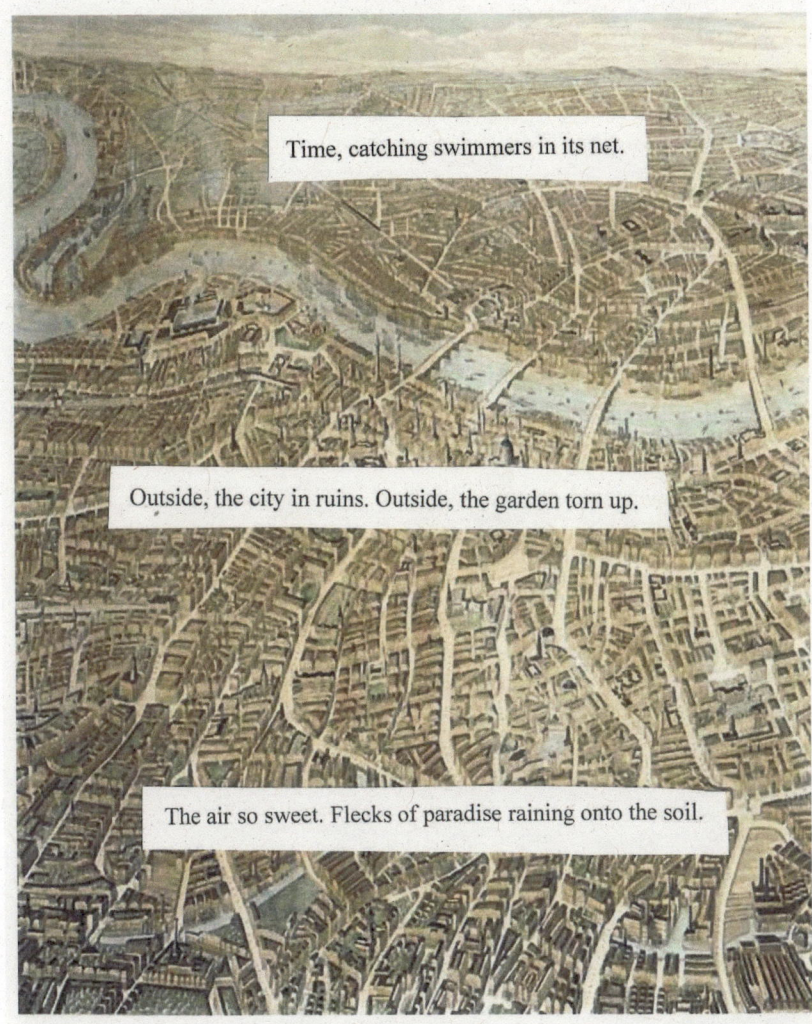

Blue Drafts (Postscript)

Maybe we wanted to drift. The ocean, Sam used to say, was the only thing louder than his tinnitus. He missed it. Madison was an isthmus but what was that compared to waves crashing?

A photo I still have—even after all these moves and the eviction when the super threw my possessions into the trash—Sam's back to the camera, head up, watching something move in the sky. Or maybe nothing.

***

I remember the clip of Bette Davis on some talk show. "Old age ain't for sissies," she said. I think of Sam and many others. Yeah, I guess not.

***

I saw Derek Jarman's *Blue* alone. The thoughts of a dying man who has lost his friends and his health and his eyesight. My fingers dug into the tatty upholstery of the armrests like I was at the dentist. I was afraid. The blue screen became a kind of hypnotist.

***

Sam lived in an extended stay motel then. Housekeeping, I said and let myself in. No one around and the bed in shambles. Strip the sheets, empty the trash, clean the bathroom. Wrote a note and stuck it to the minifridge with the magnet that read *Mummy...what is a Sex Pistol?*

We became friendly and occasionally more. Sam looked like Martin Sheen in *Badlands* and I had Sissy Spacek's deadpan voiceover playing in my head, so we made sense. He talked in his sleep sometimes and said, *I'm not here. I'm not here.*

"I was a loser with a lot going on in my head," Sam said when I asked about San Diego. I smiled. Me too. Still was. Still am.

Sam knew everything about film. He had studied it. I mean, at matinees and drive-ins and in magazines.

He worked at Four Star Video and had me over to watch movies on his VHS player. My film education: Fassbinder, Pasolini, Cassavetes, noirs, B movies, gangster pictures, midnight movies, John Waters, Richard Kern, Nick Zedd, Beth B.

Sam would argue movies with anyone. Once he heard a man refer to someone as the star of a documentary. Sam said, "The camera is the star of the documentary." The subject then, the man said. Sam nodded, unconvinced.

Jarman I knew because Sam took me to his films when they played at the Majestic or the Frederic March Play Circle in the UW Student

Union. Or they played festivals in Chicago. Queen Elizabeth I time-travels to the punk era? Sold. Then we'd go see a band at O'Cayz Corral and wake up for hair of the dog at Bennett's Smut-n-Eggs for breakfast as porn played.

* * *

Often I learned about a gay artist or writer or filmmaker by reading their obituary. They were described post-mortem as radicals, visionaries, trailblazers, pioneers. What were we left with? Mediocrities who slid into the dead's shoes and clomped around as if nothing had happened.

* * *

The smoke hurt our eyes. So many cigarettes at the parties that we hid in the bathroom with the windows open. The cold air made us cry and then laugh at our tears.

* * *

In the pandemonium of image, I present you with the universal blue. Blue, an open door to soul, an infinite possibility becoming tangible.

I didn't know what the shade of blue was called, only that as I looked at it for over an hour, it started to waver. The words spoken carried another shape, another wave, coming at you and radiating. I was emotional because I was in my body. Art did that, marked me in time. You are here.

Voices in and out. A lot of dream in there. And rage because that's waking up and sometimes falling asleep. Injustice, a word I can hardly say and no longer know how to define. I understand it a little listening to a man narrate his own disintegration. The anger moved me most because I was ashamed of mine. It was a loss of control. Girls weren't supposed to get angry. It was ugly. I wasn't a girl except everyone treated me like one. An ugly girl. Later I was the wrong man, an effeminist. I heard the anger in the words, the scrape of rage, and I was there too.

***

Static ultramarine. Marco Polo, blue-bearded death, Sarajevo, Van Gogh, Czar Ivan. Delphiniums. A recitation of side effects. Narration weaving between voices. Like a night out. Or a late night in, awake, afraid. Follow the stream of blue, a diary becomes a symphony and shifts and shifts, a garage band, a solo.

* * *

I have walked behind the sky.
For what are you seeking?
The fathomless blue of Bliss.

* * *

The list of afflictions, the suffering. All the queens dying. Regicide. And then I would work as many shifts as I could until I had money. I saved to spend it all on a ticket somewhere else, to start over. As if death wouldn't follow.

***

It started with sweats in the night and swollen glands. Then the black cancer spread across their faces—as they fought for breath, TB and pneumonia hammered their lungs, and Toxo at the brain. Reflexes scrambled—sweat poured through hair matter like lianas in the tropical forest. Voices slurred—and then were lost forever. My pen chased this story across the page tossed this way and that in the storm.

***

Nothingness. "You like that word—nothing—don't you?" Sam said one night. I guess. "You say it all the time." The void as a constant, a worry stone, a tic. I wouldn't know how to reach for the transcendental. I only wanted to sit and smoke and listen to Sam talk about movies and bands.

Sam once asked me how I could believe in nothing. How could I not? Nothingness is enormous and impossible. All that endless silence. It's beyond comprehension, much bigger than god. Nothing is everything.

I said if there were a god it would be a force that didn't answer to the word god, was not in any way anthropomorphic, most definitely was not involved in human matters, and was beyond our comprehension and even love as we understood it. The idea a force that large and abstract would love me as an individual or feel my love was absurd. And even if that force existed, I still believed my consciousness would be snuffed by my death and "I" would no longer exist. Sam was quiet, and I thought, I should start telling people I believe in god and explain it that way.

**

David ran home panicked on the train from Waterloo, brought back exhausted and unconscious to die that night. Terry mumbled incoherently into his incontinent tears. Others faded like flowers cut by the scythe of the blue-bearded reaper.

Parched as the waters of life receded, Howard turned slowly to stone. Petrified day by day, his mind imprisoned in a concrete fortress until all we could hear were his groans on the telephone, circling the globe.

The end was a long ramble A numbing list of symptoms and infections. Pneumonia. Again and again. When he was near the end, Sam was scared to be alone at night. He called me at work, hanging on the phone too long, trying to wind down and relax into sleep.

* * *

When Sam didn't pick up the phone for two days, I rang the front desk. They said they couldn't go in the room. After work, I took a cab over. As it reached the stoplight across from the motel, I saw the coroner's van pull out of the driveway.

* * *

A week later, David Robinson dumped the ashes of his partner Warren Krause on the White House grounds in protest against President George

H.W. Bush's negligence and disregard in fighting AIDS. Robinson said he was inspired by David Wojnarowicz's 1991 memoir *Close to the Knives*, which imagined "what it would be like if, each time a lover, friend or stranger died of this disease, their friends, lovers or neighbors would take the dead body and drive with it in a car a hundred miles an hour to Washington DC and blast through the gates of the White House and come to a screeching halt before the entrance and dump their lifeless form on the front steps."

***

Demarcations are form. Beginnings and endings are what grief obliterates and life tries to contain. Slippage between past and present, between one thing and another, is grief's meter. Failure is implicit. The fear of forgetting and of being forgotten, of losing still more, is the engine of grief.

The hands fall off the clock. Time becomes my mother, my brother, my friends, the people I thought I was, the girl I was, the man I slip in and out of being, a hologram. They all get placed in there. How did I become the library of everyone I love?

***

Ten degrees and everyone is smoking. I always want one when it gets this cold. Seeing breath and then seeing smoke breath, it's like weird meditation. Walking home last night was like skating and the city looked like a breathing jewel. Today it's back to windblown tundra and snow trudgery. I'm not going to take it for granted when the snow finally melts and I can take long, pointless walks again.

***

Sam taught me to pay attention to the opening and closing lines in a movie. "Sometimes they're just throwaways, but sometimes they're the poem," he said.

The sea and a chiming bell. The ending: *No one will remember our work. Our life will pass like the traces of a cloud, it will be scattered like mist that is chased by the rays of the sun. For our time is the passing of a shadow. Our lives will run like sparks through the stubble. I place a delphinium, blue, upon your grave.*

The opening lines: *Love is life and love lasts forever. My heart's memory turns to you*, David, Howard, Graham, Terry, Paul...

Joe, Kevin, Toby, Sam....

Nate Lippens

David David—
Dav—
David David David David David David David David
David David—
David David David David Dav—
David David—

Howard Howard Howard Howard—
Howard Howard Howard Howard Howard Howard Howard
How—
Howard Howard Howard Howard Howard Howard Howard
Howard Howard Howard How—
How—
Howard Howard Howard Howard Howard Howard Howard
Howard Howard—
Howard Howard—

Graham Graham Graham Graham Graham Graham Graham—
Graham Graham Graham Graham Graham Graham Graham
Graham Graham Graham Graham Graham Graham Graham
Graham Grahm Graham Graham—

"kiss me aga—
in" a—
voice in Blue says "kiss me, kiss me again, and again...never
enough" Blu—
e never goes i hope to stay the—
same color w—

hen i die i hope to leave through—
words in mouths this morning, i let in Blue light through my
nostr—
ils i breathe in Blue light let out more Blue i imagine writing
his name in slim Blue iridesce—
nt cu—
rves on my chest thighs eyes & eyelids: Kenny Kenny Kenny
Kenny Kenny Ke—
nny Kenny Kenn—

y Kenny Kenny Kenny Kenny Kenny Kenny Kenny Kenny—
Kenny Kenny Kenny Kenny Kenny Kenny Kenny Ke
nny Kenny Kenny Kenny Kenny Kenny Kenny Kenny
Kenny Ken did not die of aids th—

Graham—
Graham Graham Graham Graham Graham Graham Graham
Graham—
Graham—
Graham Graham Graham Graham Graham Graham Graham
Graham Graham Graham Graham Graham Graham—

Terry Terry Terry Terry Terry Terry Terry Terry Terry Terry
Terry—
Terry Terry Ter—
Terry Terry Terry Terry Terry Terry Terry Terry Terry—
Terry Terry Terry Terry Terry Terry Terry Terry Terry—
Terry Terry Terry Terry Terry Terry Terry Terry Terry
Terry Terry Ter—

Paul Paul Paul Paul Paul Paul Paul Paul Paul Paul Paul
Paul Paul Paul Paul—
Paul—
Paul Paul Paul Paul Paul Paul Paul Paul Paul Paul Paul
Paul Paul Paul Paul Paul Paul Paul Paul—
Paul Paul Paul Paul Paul Paul Paul Paul Paul Paul Paul—

ough he—
is present in my diary of Blue a perhaps soulmate stands beside the pilla—
r of Dere—
k's lost Blue friends they are all dead now - a palette knife e
venly spreads the same digital Blue i made a home i—

n the names of friends chanted softly: David, Howard, Graham, Terry,—
Paul, David, i ca—
nnot look at the Blue for long. i see your eyes openin—
g and closing. the same Blue life taking up your vision—
, Howard, Graham, Terry, Ross, counting each name, we ex
tend Blue we m—

ake more life with more breath. "do you see the sun rise & the sun set?" the int—
ervi—
ewer asks. "i do" Derek says, mouth pursed, smiling: "the s
un comes up at the front of the house and it—
goes down at the back. and i see the sun all day if it's there."—

Jason Lipeles

BLU / R

I

the sky is blue > the sea is blue > your eyes are blue > my lies are blue > my bruises blue > my heart is blue > my mind is blue > my blood is blue > my veins blue river > under skin > translucent > transcendent > transmogrified > blue > this space is blue > this liminal place > this transportation > from one thing belonging to another > transition blue > collision of metaphors > stream of unconsciousness > a journey up river > into heart of blue darkness > moon > rhapsody > velvet > shoes > all is blue > eyes > skies > bayou blue > the red and the white > and the baby blue > collar > christmas > joni blue > pale blue > black and blue > highway room > island lights > fluorescent blue > electric blue > blue blue electric blue > roses are red > violence is blue > midnight > monday > royal blue > heaven blue > true blue > clear blue >

II

the morning the line came back as clear > blue > and a blue week later > the HIV test came back as negative > blue > his jeans were blue > his eyes were blue > his smile was blue > his hands > his hips > his lips were blue > our hotel was blue > his room was blue > the bed was blue > did we blue kiss? > I don't recall blue > but we fucked blue > 'til blue in the morning > face blue > in the morning > I faced the consequences blue > of our blue-drunk blue-sex > no protection blue > we sung the blues > and you shook me all night long >

III

the Earth is blue > is beautiful blue > is essentially blue > life-giving > plant-living blue > hue > aquamarine > ultramarine > turquoise > teal > sapphire > cyan > indigo > azure > cerulean > gentian > heliotrope > lapis lazuli > buddha is blue > mohammed is blue > jesus cobalt christ is blue > god is blue > my god is a blue field > of vision > inside a blue bag > of hopelessness > missed opportunities > my loss is blue > my life is blue > your death > is blue

IV

The war rages across the newspapers
Another year is passing
I hear the voices of dead friends
Awareness is heightened by this
My room has welcomed many summers
Here I am again in the waiting room
I am always here before the doors open
There is a photo in the newspaper of refugees
The demented woman switching the channels on the TV
I have a sinking feeling in my stomach
The worst of the illness is uncertainty
The sound of feet rushing along the corridor
His groans on the telephone circling the globe
Munching through a packet of dry biscuits
Digging can only proceed on the calmest of days
The sea of years and the timeless ocean
The mirrors reflect each of your betrayals
Closeted and frightened by my sexuality
It started with sweats in the night
We all contemplated suicide
Cum splattered nuclear breeders
Cross-eyed meddlesome consciousness
I gag on them as I swallow them
Blood lines and blood banks
Travelling to Berlin with a fridge under my arm
As I slept a jet slammed into a tower block
No entrances or exits now

Time is what keeps the light from reaching us
So the rich and powerful who fucked us over fuck us over again
The earth is dying and we do not notice it
The earth is dying and we do not notice it
The earth is dying and *still* we do not notice it
If you are concerned about any of the above side-effects, please ask your doctor
The shoes I am wearing should be sufficient to walk me out of life
The room is full of men and women squinting into the dark
The shattering bright light
I step off the kerb

JP Seabright

Jarman's breath

'Voice of God': the name given to a narrative style typically associated with 'classical' documentary films of the 1930s and 40s. An authoritative, omniscient, and disembodied voice—heard as white, male, and middle-class—instructs and guides us through the images. It is *acousmatic*: it comes to us as if from behind a veil and its source remains unseen, redoubling its authority.

Jarman relishes the sacred and the sacrilegious. He might be pleased, then, that his narration of *Blue* evokes and contorts the 'Voice of God'. He says *room* as *rum* and *lump* as *lamp*; in his plummy pronunciation I hear his South-of-England upbringing, his time at prep schools, public schools, boarding schools. White, male, and middle-class: it is a voice I'm conditioned to think of as authoritative. This acousmatic voice is concealed behind a veil of International Klein Blue, but it is far from disembodied. The voice, Mladen Dolar tells us, is an extension of the breath, *the zero point of vocal emission*. Here the voice puffs and pants, it whispers and susurrates, a cacophony of plosives and sibilants and affricates. The words almost buried under the weight of his breath. Jarman's breath.

*

My vision will never come back, the voice confesses. *The virus rages fierce*. The film's single, ultramarine frame supposedly reflects the loss of Jarman's sight as a result of an AIDS-related illness. But Jarman tells also of the deterioration of voice and breath suffered by his friends and lovers—a fate he knows, we know, awaits him. *As they fought for breath, TB and pneumonia hammered at the lungs, and Toxo at the brain. ... Voices slurred—and then they were lost forever. Blue* was screened for the first time in June 1993. Jarman died less than a year later.

In *Blue*, the voice scurries, propelled by the breath. It darts through and around syllables, almost tripping, as if trying to outrun the fate it describes. And then, with the meditative chiming of a bell, the breath slows. The breath grounds. *Fate is the strongest. Fate, fated, fatal. I resign myself to fate.* The voice croons, spins tales both fantastic and mundane, tales of love and sex and lapis lazuli. The breath grows shallow, it quickens. Then another quip, and the cycle begins again. *The Gautama Buddha instructs me to walk away from illness—but he wasn't attached to a drip.* The back-and-forth between resistance to, resignation towards, and acceptance of life's transience is marked by the rhythms and cadences of breath.

*

Blue is a transformative documentary ... in which the process of dying is hashed out with pathos (Benjamin Bennett-Carpenter). If *Blue* is a documentary, then Jarman's voice and his breath are its invisible documents. José Muñoz describes the 'vexed' relationship of queerness to visible evidence: *leaving too much of a trace has often meant that the queer subject has left herself open for attack.* A visible subject is easier to discipline. Photographs of emaciated bodies—Peter Hujar and David Kirby and countless others—constitute a moving, if complicated, archive of images responding to the invisibility of AIDS in public discourse, particularly in the 1980s and 90s. But Jarman's breath—while perhaps inseparable from this archive—offers an alternative. An invisible and elusive archive; an archive that speaks to an experience of AIDS at the end of the twentieth century under a Tory government in England; an archive nonetheless wilfully and deliciously open to flights of fancy, fantasy, and desire. The voice is archive. The breath is archive.

*

Jarman's voice creaks, it trills, it sings. In the glow of the absolute blue, the contours of the voice become more insistent. The blue of meditation: an invitation to breathe. *Our name will be forgotten in time ... Our life will pass like the traces of a cloud.*

His voice barely a whisper, his breath traces a line along my neck, up towards my ear, then my scalp. It tingles. I am alive. *The universal blue.*

Andrew Cummings

Sig Olson

Prophecy

Almost before it started blue the snow was gone
stunning and crystalline into a post-it written over
your mother's shoulder, I walked across the river
and south to read with you at the bookshop where
a cake was served, cherry-chocolate and we coughed
from the new rain, it coloured our voices in the poems
and watered our throats with diesel and sugar. Having swept
away everything, the snow knew our shame and its melt
revealed holes. As if not to speak of them
we continued to think about Yorkshire, the power gone out
in the hills our train would sluice, as we cut away excess
curlicues from the tomato plant on Montague Street
baroque in how it had almost died from the effort of its own
abundance, a sole fruit left on the vine
where you had sat, swollen with mornings
and the dream of where to go with the feeling of
anything over. As if to speak risqué
for the want of vitamins, the note dissolved also
in the amnesia of waking to know our bodies
are merely warm mammals: one is cadmium,
the other aquamarine as I do not want
to leave the bed's dialectics, wetly encased in cellophane
and held for centuries in the cryosphere of our hardcore
so that if I leave here, twirling the swab around my tonsils
you will remember my ass and the hibiscus
architecture witnesses the missing, in the ossuary of other forms
our amazing exits are open until they are blue in the face
as the trees were nude until somebody painted them, blue
telling the other trees they were sick. I am positive.

No one really dreams any longer of the Blue Flower

And now become fact
it grows in your lungs
many kinds of socialism or breakfast
petalled and fractal insubstance
the rarest of all flowers is the blue apology
slipped into the mouth of the red post box slyly
nostalgic for fiction
like I tell you
a dream, and it burns

*title is taken from Walter Benjamin's essay 'Dream Kitsch'

Maria Sledmere

Portara

Look, the full throat of the sky.
One cool blue gullet.
And in it, me. A few steps
Too far up a slippery slope.
It's just I see a window to god
And simply must be pressed up against it.
Also, there is dogwood crushed

Between the pages of my passport.
An attempt, I explain
As the alarm bells are raised.
I know it's not an attractive trait–
To scrabble up on your table,
Pressed to a celluloid jerky.
But I have no friends who are not dying.

Cleo Henry

BLUE

"the great thing about the sea is it changes every colour you can imagine — i've seen the sea pink and brown and cream black"

jesus fuck christ i'm so sorry
together take a blue from jarman
i'll treat this grief like the dodgems too
bang bang skid
damn
remember you as (immobile) chemical lab too
D keeping count with a hand-drawn spreadsheet
you always loved jarman
his darling, his garden
and popping prescriptions pills

as i lie on the sofa
re-swimming in blue
i understand something more about
the visits to the whittington
the coughing, the drips, the tubes
why you wanted to go to the zoo
(the what? the zoo?) for your (what we didn't know then but was the last) birthday

but you're not here to say yes or
hmm no, not really
not here to corroborate this lighthouse-grieving of mine
so maybe there's no same
at all

how is it i think that you, a cis-het white women, introduced me to so many queers M?

in some ways, you are my
dyke-on-a-fucking-motorbike
isn't that wild

Jessie McLaughlin

Blue, or the remnants of a disease

My blue was not dangerous, did not demand attention, was not edgy. My blue offered me a place in the background. My blue was, as a teenager, a safe choice. It was the colour of a memory or a daydream. These were my days of gazing out of classrooms windows, listening with half an ear. Not being too eager, not gesticulating too much while talking. My years of slinking out of classrooms unnoticed, roaming the hallways, biking home. I'd pass through pastures in the twilight and watch the mist rise from the ditches. A group of boys in the distance, *like a blue frost it caught them.* I witnessed someone else's memories, heralded by a singing bowl: a monochrome blue illuminated the bicycle path. *The virus rages fierce. I have no friends now who are not dead or dying. No one will remember our work.* The group was ambushed by colour; they trimmed their laughter down to a murmur. The weak glow of their taillights converged, like hands seeking each other in the dark. *Kiss me on the lips, on the eyes. Our name will be forgotten in time.* Some of the boys said goodbye, the group fell apart. One remained. I rose out of my saddle to break into a sprint. I wanted to be with him, but the blue caught up with me.

My art history professor stands in front of the class, pointing at the slide display. A streak of sunlight cleaves a tone of blue, as in Barnett Newman's *Cathedra*. The curtains in the back of the room aren't fully closed. Throughout the class, the image remains blurred. *All the best film directors were originally painters,* the professor says proudly, as though he had contributed to the film himself. *What does this blue image remind you of?* Nobody raises their hands. I don't think of AIDS, as I later will. We are shown a film fragment and a tired voice asks: *How are we perceived, if we are to be perceived at all? For the most part, we are invisible.* My professor does not linger on the work for long. The film is a visual appetiser for a PowerPoint full of black-and-white photographs. Our interest oozes out of the classroom and the whispers gather strength. There will have been a moment that my professor mentions a cause of death. He will not have failed to note that the artist was a homosexual. The group of boys in the back will not have failed to laugh and howl. I underline Derek Jarman's name in my art history book. The film is not on the exam.

The text of *Blue* was originally a chapter in Jarman's book *Chroma*. In it, the artist – by then as good as blind – explores the personal and historical connotations of various colours. The irony of this undertaking does not prevent him from carrying out his task with playful erudition. Every colour is treated with equal love and dedication, and much like the film, the book is filled with references to Greek tragedies, English poets, and trysts. Reading *Chroma* means undulating between Jarman's idealised England and the political situation he decries. As I read it, I am reminded of just how easy it can be to forget how radical his generation of artists was. The book was written *at the hind end of those Thatcher years of Conservative ideology*, notes Ali Smith in her introduction, *one of outright persecution and conscious marginalisation of the queer community in the midst of what was a full-on and tragic catastrophe, the AIDS epidemic.* The government did not do much to come to Jarman's aid; his less-famous comrades could only count on its complete neglect. Legislation like Section 28 and the ongoing stigmas surrounding the disease would have caused many an HIV patient to lose hope. When Jarman turns to the political realities of his era in *Blue*, he says sardonically: *Three quarters of the AIDS organisations are not providing safer sex information. One district said they had no queers in their community, but you might try district X, they have a theatre.*

I don't believe we ended up actually watching *Blue* in art history class, or in any class at all that year. All we got was that fragment, after which the conversation moved on to abstract expressionism and the work of colour field painters. I don't think that can be blamed on my professor's lack of willingness to leave the beaten path; in retrospect, the reason must have been the substance of the film. Because if *Blue* had been shown in full that day, I'm positive it would have left a lasting mark on my classmates. I watched the film later, in the safety of my bedroom, where I had my first personal encounter with a role model whose life was not defined by machismo. Here was an artist who chose to spend the end of his life planting a garden near a nuclear power plant. Here was an artist who chose pleasure and friendship over toughness and stoicism. *Civilisation is queer,* Jarman announces in his diary. *From the moment Lorenzo, who slept with boys, commissioned Ficino to translate Plato, things changed.*

In his films, I saw the men I learned about in school, Caravaggio, Wittgenstein, fall in love with other men. Jarman's teachings began to form a parallel curriculum, centring on the love life of artists. Through the histories he narrated for me, and by offering me his own life as an example, he enabled me to identify alternative ways to shape my masculinity. In high school, however, the activism of Jarman's position and his work will have escaped me. I will not have been aware of how eagerly the tabloid press embraced him as a tool to push their reactionary agenda. At the end of *Blue*, a men's choir claps and cheers loudly, as if we suddenly find ourselves in a soccer match. They chant: *I am a cock sucking / Straight acting / Lesbian man / With ball crushing bad manners / Laddish nymphomaniac politics / Spunky sexist desires / of incestuous invesrsion and / Incorrect terminology / I am a Not Gay.*

Why was Blue *not angrier?* The answer is quite simple: *I really don't feel angry, just melancholy, so* Blue *is a true aspect of my state of mind. I don't wake up in the morning fizzing with fury.* Jarman's diary, published posthumously as *Smiling in Slow Motion*, covers his everyday life until his very last days, including his attendance at *Blue's* 1993 premiere at the New York Film Festival. He writes that he received one solitary interesting question from a journalist. His answer betrays a deeply polite personality. In the film's most personal moments, Jarman summons the dead: the names of his lovers *David, Howard, Graham, Terry, Paul* form the refrain of his visual swan song. The melancholy that Jarman speaks of resembles what art historian Douglas Crimp describes as militant mourning, in which unresolved grief is transformed into a source of activist strength. Reading and watching old queer content also evokes a kind of wistfulness in me, a sense that the possibility of a different kind of world, one shaped by this generation of artists, has passed away along with them. Is Jarman's utopian perspective – one he shared with countless other artists – still one that inspires activists? Or is ours a time of cultural and historical gentrification, as Sarah Schulman suggests?

I ask myself if Jarman would have been canonised, had it not been for his premature death. *Blue* could hardly be called a success. A respected reviewer of the Dutch public broadcasting service wrote upon its release that *only a handful of film fanatics will make it to the end. While there are evidently admirers who deify this British director, still, this is altogether too much.* Today, the film is seen as one of the trailblazing releases of the twentieth century and showered in commentary and analysis. It is more commonly seen in museums than in cinemas. And this carries the risk that the film's content is reduced to a moment in history: the AIDS epidemic as a time on which we look back. As film theorist So Mayer writes, *when it is pinned in the gallery, no one has to listen to the formidable soundtrack, only drift past the lightbox-like screen. In being only seen within that frame – without its context, including knowledge of the liveness of its original performance – the film's power is diminished and contained.* In interviews, and especially in his memoirs, Jarman resists the way his sexuality was stripped of sex, by the media as well as by well-intentioned interest groups. It is always sex and connection, a radical hedonism, that is at the heart of Jarman's work, even in the apparently sexless *Blue*.

In the basement of the Stedelijk Museum Amsterdam, one can find Yves Klein's canvas *L'accord bleu (RE 10)*. Looking at the work, I can sense how my experience of it is manipulated. The intensity of the pigment, the International Klein Blue, pulls away my gaze from other paintings. The work absorbs my full attention, like the sponges that are mounted to it. The Stedelijk's website describes the work as a lunar landscape, an alien combination of colour and texture. The sponges form a kind of craters, surrounded by moonstones. This high-flying explanation propels my gaze towards the stars, but the irregularities of the painting's texture sooner remind me of big moles, or warts. The edges of the canvas are grainy, flaking like eczema. If I apply this human perspective to International Klein Blue, the canvas seems to me to centre Klein himself: it is 'his' blue that insists on my concern. Where Klein could have shown a human figure, he opts for a self-portrait in close-up instead. It is here that *Blue*'s use of International Klein Blue diverges from that of the canvas: the film doesn't draw us in, but rather illuminates the faces of the viewers and forms a connection with them. The colour projects itself outwards, turning its observers into personal witnesses of the story it has to tell.

On Instagram, art gallery David Zwirner proudly announced last summer that Derek Jarman's later work, including *Blue*, would be part of their new permanent exhibition. For emphasis, we are given an image of Jarman staring straight into the camera with wide-open, bloodshot eyes, embedded in mounds of flesh that reminds me of Klein's sponges. Amidst the outpouring of celebratory comments, someone asks: *what is such an impossibly wealthy institution like @davidzwirner doing to address the political urgency of AIDS today? What is @davidzwirner doing to support the radical queer political agenda that Jarman fought for tirelessly?*

Lars Meijer

I met Derek on Old Compton Street one afternoon when I was nineteen. I was at a low point in my young life. I'd moved to England with vague plans of going to film school, but the relatives I was living with had thrown me out of their home after catching me watching a late night broadcast of *The Garden* on Channel 4. I was so engrossed that I didn't hear the creak on the staircase. The lights flicked on and things went to hell. The only scene they'd witnessed was of two men gently kissing in a bath. It was my first acquaintance with the term "bender" – typed out the word looks quaint, not the caustic thing that hit my ears. I'd been reading *Modern Nature* and it buoyed me as I hauled my luggage around London, looking for somewhere to stay. I knew that I was participating in a painful, but age-old arc of queer life: rebuke, exile, and the search for the new garden. I had been shoved off a path that wasn't mine to inherit anyway. From then on it was changed priorities ahead: new horizons only.

Thanks to a noticeboard in a queer café I found work (that barely paid) and a bedsit in a gay household (that I could barely afford). I was broke, and the only reason I ran into Derek in the first place was that I'd fainted from hunger on the job and been given the day off. As I blearily wandered around the gay neighbourhood, wondering if things would ever be okay, I spotted Derek on the street squinting through his glasses. Like some other men I knew, he was going blind from the AIDS drugs he was taking. When I approached him he was friendly (I made a point of saying that I was a Canadian film student, knowing his first love was a Canadian boy) and he invited me to join him on his errands. He said he was concerned that his failing eyesight might lead him to stumble into the road and I offered him my arm. He directed us into the back of a delicatessen to sample olives from the huge barrels the owner opened especially for him. When I declined to try them he cried, "Oh! My dear, you must develop a taste for olives!" And then tried not to look embarrassed as I started wolfing down handfuls.

He wanted to get his hair cut next, and asked me to come along. I sat at the foot of an antique barber chair while he told the hairdresser about his plan to write a book on colour; he said it seemed like a sensible thing to do before he went completely blind. I knew of his stoic side from his journals, but his matter-of-factness threw me. What surprised me more was that he advised me, several times that afternoon, to abandon any idea of becoming a filmmaker and to concentrate on being an artist instead. "You wouldn't like where it's all headed," he told me. The underground that had sustained him and his peers was vanishing, the communal aspect of movie-going likewise ebbing away. Derek's one proviso, if I ever did make a film, was that it should be about my friends.

In his books, as in *Blue*, Derek describes the sore-covered sallow cheeks, swollen bellies and vacant eyes of young men wasting away from the disease – not as an observer, but as one of the fallen. Given charity but no real compassion from the public, its political and religious emissaries allowed to heap further torment on every deathbed, as they tried to persuade the stricken that the disease was a heavenly indictment of their 'lifestyle'. How could a filmmaker possibly bracket the endless, bitter weeping of outcasts who had found new families, and were now forced to bury them? How to deliver a testament to people who may not want, or can't bear, to hear it?

I ran into Derek a few more times, fleetingly, in the year before I went back to Canada to enroll in art school. I watched *Edward II* and *Wittgenstein*, and wondered if he'd exaggerated his disillusionment with filmmaking: here were two more masterpieces. It was only when I encountered some of his paintings, and after I'd finally seen *Blue*, that I understood. Film and video are too of-this-world to lead us out of it. As inexorably lashed to the minutes and seconds as we are, film unwinds towards its end, made to neatly wrap up things that aren't neat, tack endings on to the on-going, feign resolution where none exists: "Time is what keeps the light from reaching us." How then to fix your passion and your fury – unchanging, fulgurating and accusatory – in midair? The magician dissolves film-time into painting-time, and leads us out of the maelstrom.

Blue is, of course, a film about disease and blindness and death, but it's no headstone. It does what painting can sometimes do, or what Jarman hoped queerness might achieve: it proposes the obliteration of horizons. In its place, open space for new vistas, new kinds of intrepidness and doubt can begin to bloom. You need to watch *Blue* with both friends and strangers so you all dissolve together in its lapis glow, so that you get a taste of the shimmering, nameless thing that underpins the whole of experience: not emptiness but a plenum void. The dust and scratches flicker past on the film's surface (I once experienced a print of the film so worn with play, it looked like it would disintegrate before my eyes) yet the blue remains, vast, luminous and unperturbed. You might glean an understanding of why Jarman felt that queer people were especially deft at gilding the path towards it – voyagers with no particular home and little to lose. At the end, when even sight is gone, what's left? After loss and defeat, what remains? Rage. Then tenderness. Illimitable space, more than enough room to embrace strangeness and uncertainty; all the anger and sadness, just curious points on the provisional maps we lay down over the oddity of being alive. Love stays when the map is dissolved – it's all that remains of queerness when the bodies that propel and compel us are taken out of the equation. Queer love: the entropic bolt we must bring, again and again, to shake up and shatter those frozen, worn out systems.

> "Blue – stretches, yawns, and is awake…
> infinite possibility becoming tangible….
> kiss me again, and again."

Scott Treleaven

ganzfeld dream

a suggestion: stare at the text. do not read. receive a message. then respond.

having been starved of physical contact we meet in front of the painting where we kiss soft & long after sharing the paradox of intimacy at a distance. like something from a film but was not a film. was more, how to say this: a childhood memory? he said: epistolary relationships always feel like i'm writing to myself. all around was static that shook our senses into a hum of pleasure. all the colours bleeding between us. all our raw adolescence bubbling up—the warmth of a bath. we met to learn about Seurat, because of Sondheim, because of mutual ignorance, because of a collaborative wish to have our minds fisted, because we are arse licking psycho fags who ball lesbian boys, because how else to continue while loved ones are dying? we stop kissing one another & begin licking the frame of the Bathers at Asnières. we smell the wood & wonder who had been the last to do so—was their scent still here? i tickle the dog & kiss the train. he pulls out his cock, fingers his foreskin & traces the words on the label. large. rejected. men. absorbed. suffused. frozen. the bathers invite us to remove our clothing. now my torso is bare, dick out & i begin to piss a stream of blue. he kneels before me & i fill his mouth, paint his face, splash his pearly chest with dark blue to make a model out of him. we are in the entire field of our leisure where the questions are yet to be formulated—bathing in the blue of disorientation. he turns to face the men in the frame, trousers around ankles, a jock bearing his cheeks, offering his hole, which becomes a cornflower, a cyan bachelor's button. looking up at the bathers he begs them to deprive him of all dryness. the men stand, take out their differently flaccid cocks & shower him along with me. he rolls in the growing puddle of ultramarine, his cock flowing too, a fountain high enough to reach my mouth. when he speaks i can't hear what he is saying through the hopelessly impressionistic ecology of our relation. but moving to lie next to him i drink the fluid message he attempts to communicate. hold it in my mouth. we are damp, together—sodden with our inner blue. splashes of piss & paint spread out across the gallery & begin to pool around the feet of other visitors. for a moment i think i see Bridget Riley, but am taken away from any distinct recognition while we fuck & buck & dance, becoming lines, dots, marks. fading out until all the pleasure of our bodies shakes the room into a vibration of oceanic proportions such that the water from the Seine begins to spill out of the painting, flooding the room, sweeping us up, drowning all promise, submerging our desire, extinguishing the future, engulfing every sense, murdering total being. the bliss of blue blue blue

Declan Wiffen

Harry Agius

after *Blue* (1993)

a thin cigarette aloft out of the brown open window, the dark room fizzes in spectral light. oh give me your vibration, silence - symphony. an unpocketed peppermint, stripes like the cat, rolls around my tongue while i consider the slicing of opacified lenses.

i'm too sore a loser to play chess, i'm too torrential to be able to plan four or five moves ahead. yesterday the year slips on the calendar and today i have cool marble knuckles. instead, i watch Emily and Camille hungover in the Jean Cocteau chapel in St. Tropez.

thank you for your kind attention, there is a large damp watercolour shut up in your drawer. what can i do? stop now? i have walked behind the sky, pencils, noses, movies, legs, the fathomless bliss. your japanese jacket settles with the ardent moths who have recently claimed the fingertips of my left glove.

Caitlin Merrett King

1

the sodomite had been a temporary aberration; the homosexual was now a spieces. (FOUCAULT)

the prophet is meeting us at the garden.
garden of luxury - eden - tortures.
rave-war microverse
beautiful and or but industrial machinic love is pushed to the limits. haemo-poetic machines of desire reproductive of sounds, like a clock (biological).

two trees coincide with each other in desire/two hares coincide with each other's meals/two friends coincide with each other in thought

this is a dream i had. immortality of the flesh means never fading chromo-structures but it also means the extension of perceptive time fabrications.

deathless symptoms,

interior androgyny, a hermaphroditism of the soul. (FOUCAULT)

Loss of signal.

2

But the iron chains held him firmly. Tongues of fire twisted around his body, hissing:
"Everything repeats itself!" (BOGDANOV)

TWICE THE PROSPECT OF FUTURABILITY, ANTI-DECAY OF THE FLESH POSTPONED: THIS IS MY MORTAL ANNOUNCEMENT.

From the diary of the one who eats:

I look up but see nothing but dark. Tremble in fear, vertiginous or lonely - dense. Shiver, but this time, the body is speaker, sound diffuses from my cells. Onward. Every vein the veil that displays my faith. The screen in front of me has been blue all along.

From the diary of the one who is eaten:

Stay put, keep on, hard as muscle, death like the empire 5th, crave holes, cave dreams. Forgotten mythologies, hummus - humified flesh made garden once more. Loss of sight, all is but surface.

ALL IS FLUX (HERACLITUS)

António Manso Preto

new tautology

going, going, gone
for what is losing half a sight to a filmmaker?

someone once told me a movie could be as easy
as a title and ninety minutes of *something* to show for it.
so a dance could be not lifting a finger and
literature a string of syllables. a defining object
of the century a urinal, signed.
art, then, is defined by defiance.

i am struck by the elegant plays of stubbornness.
like the boy in my aesthetics class
who asked,
is sport not art too? vilified as not understanding
of the subject, he simply questioned
as if his life depended on it.
vision is leaning against everything,
seeing beyond the geography of limits

Adriana Lazarova

SITUATED BLISS

"So, not so perversely, objectivity turns out to be about particular and specific embodiment and definitely not about the false vision promising transcendence of all limits and responsibility...Feminist objectivity is about limited location and situated knowledge, not about transcendence and splitting of subject and object. It allows us to become answerable for what we learn how to see."

—Donna Haraway, "Situated Knowledges: The Science Question in Feminism and the Privilege of Partial Perspective" (1988).

At age 9 one of my fave effeminate alchemist hermit bachelors was: Isaac Newton. Nature or Nurture? I *was* an effeminate alchemist hermit bachelor, but it might actually have been my dad's idea to do a project that historically reenacted Newton's optical experiments, called "WHY IS THE SKY BLUE?" because, dad said: *don't you want to learn about your favourite colour?*

WHY IS THE SKY BLUE? An experiment by Brooke Palmieri.
I'd had to work really hard for Blue: *Blue is for Boys*, each teacher dating back to preschool at Church of the Atonement in 1992, had told me. Blue was taken away from me in whatever form it took—toys, crayons, blankets, baseball caps, bicycles—other boys could just wear it, have stuff in blue, no problem. And now: I had to do a bunch of reading and experiments and then write them out on a cardboard triptych for a competitive "science fair"? Really? I didn't notice that any other kid had to justify their tastes this way, but I suspect that all of them did. This isn't a coming out narrative to distinguish myself as queer and different from the other kids—that's an adult story that comes later—what I'm saying is that in the glorious weirdness of primordial ooze that is childhood, I was, probably like the others, never just left to *be* but had to learn a lot of different strategies to get away

with *just being*. Like I think my dad was trying to say: *They can't take the colour of the sky from you, so go with that, learn how to love in ways that they can't take away.*

On the other hand: Is this my first experience of having to work within The Scientific Establishment to describe, discipline, defend my desires? Most Likely. Would they let blue be my favourite colour if I told them it was because I loved the colour of the sky rather than—for example— because I wanted to find the ooze from Dimension X that would let me become my Teenage Mutant Ninja Turtle action figure, Leonardo, and wear a blue bandana? Barely. Would I, for the next two decades, continue to turn every interest into a meticulous research project in order to justify my most base inclinations? Absolutely.

***

This was the experiment: order a glass prism from the National Geographic Seasonal Gift Catalogue. Once the prism comes in the mail, get an old shoebox, paint the inside black, wrap the outside in the classiest leftover Christmas wrapping paper you can find, cut a slit to shine a flashlight through, and experiment with shifting the prism at different angles and distances from the light. Find the best position from which to separate the single beam of light into a rainbow. You need to cut another little hole in the box to peep through to see the results, too.

People will be able to use this box to do the experiment for themselves at the fair, to begin the initiation rites that will lead to a devotion to Blue. For the display: draw a landscape imagining little raindrops and molecules in the sky as an infinitude of prismatic forms, turning beams of the sun into rainbows. Then draw diagrams about the wavelengths of each colour, how blue and violet have the shortest wavelengths so get *scattered* during the day when the sun is high in the sky. Why don't we see a violet sky? It's biased to say the sky is blue, because human eyes are more sensitive to picking up blue light. *Why is the sky blue?* Because you're a human, we're all human, it's nice to have some things in common and other things not in common, fun. Draw a green alien in the corner with purple sunglasses to represent extraterrestrial vision. Draw your little dog Champ, in the other corner to reference alternative terrestrial vision (Champ will be the chief participant in next year's experiment: "How Are Dogs Like Wolves?"). At sunset, when the sun is lower and its white hot light has to travel further through the atmosphere, the sky appears in a fiery rage of reds and oranges—the triptych began with sunrise, was taken up by high noon, and concludes with just this kind of sunset. Great project, but it only got an honourable mention, a purple ribbon, not a blue one. The judge's own son got first prize, which my dad took really personally. My parents didn't have time to be involved at the school, they were too busy working jobs they hated. *It's rigged*, he said in disgust, *There's no such thing as merit. It's all rigged.*

* * *

Derek Jarman's *Blue* is prismatic in its own way. A blue scattered from the spectrum of colours he discusses in his last book, *Chroma*, the first book of his I'd ever encountered in a moment when I felt completely alone as a queer deeply invested in Renaissance philosophy & history. I'm talking humours, alchemy, angelic conversations, I didn't relate to the *epistemology of the closet*, and here was Derek Jarman reading that stuff too, all across his diaries, and of course partying, just like me. The narration of *Blue* is just one deeply personal chapter of *Chroma*—we met each other in that color from two very different ends of a spectrum made possible by our words, our limited locations. His chapter comes toward the end of a vigorous/rigorous mix of memoir and quotation —"Into the Blue"—nestled between chapters on "Leonardo" (not the Ninja Turtle) and "Isaac Newton." Extremes of sex and chastity. On Da Vinci: *He liked rude boys who stole, rough diamonds, like Salai who came as an assistant at fifteen and stayed for life. Leonardo's sex life was active and open enough for complaints by outraged citizens.* On Newton: *White light shattered into colour, Isaac in his closet, married to his prism and gravity with a little alchemy on the side.* When "Into the Blue" was filtered from out of *Chroma* and revised and written into its own notebook, it was given a new title: *A Blueprint for Bliss...A dialogue between* THE ARTIST & ST RITA OF CASCIA, *Patron St of LOST CAUSES*. Only later it would be simplified: *Blue*.

***

We visited the shrine of St. Rita when I was 10 or 11—our class got to take a bus into Philly for the trip—and I remember the fear that was also excitement, my heart racing as I walked up to the statue of her in holy ecstasy, surrounded by hundreds of roses, to leave an offering—a quarter or two in a box. My greatest fear at that age was the gift of the stigmata. I'd had nightmares about it—or were they prophetic dreams? I was a good kid, but I'd started to commit little sins on purpose, like telling lies or coveting things, to try to keep from being *too good*, since being really good was what got you the stigmata. In one lie, I said my favourite color was red.

***

On the cover of *A Blueprint for Bliss* a square fragment of glass was mounted and engraved by Jarman, reading: BLISS.

I think of John Donne in "A Valediction of My Name, In the Window": *My name engraved herein/ Doth contribute my firmness to this glass,/ Which ever since that charm hath been/ As hard, as that which graved it was.*

Sophomore year, March 2007, I wrote in "The Peculiarities of a Window Pane: Glass, Rank, and John Donne's Love Poetry in Early Modern England," that "Scarcity increases value, and in 16th century England, glass was a rarity." John Donne couldn't afford the pane of glass he was vandalising, that mattered to me. But what strikes me most now about the poem is the intense magic of Donne's engraving, it's a love spell: *Till my return repair/ and recompact my scatter'd body so,/ As all the virtuous powers which are/ Fix'd in the stars are said to flow/ Into such characters as gravéd be/ When these stars have supremacy.* His scattered body, it has power, maybe more power than it does when he's *there*. Until Donne returns to his lover's bedroom where he has scratched that name, the characters of his name draw down the the heavens, very hermetic, but also creepy like the lyrics to "You Oughta Know," by Alanis Morissette—*Every time I scratch my nails/Down someone else's back I hope you feel it*. Different surface, same vibe, scratching as a type of channelling energy into a surface, then releasing it. In other stanzas the engraved name has the ability to: summon Donne's reflection, never be erased, make Donne's lover mourn his absence daily, and overshadow the name of anyone else his lover may try to write letters to, or bring to bed.

I imagine these occult powers of reflection, refraction, restriction, revision as embedded in Jarman's engraving of *BLISS*, too. He knew his Donne: "The Sun Rising" is mounted on the side of Prospect Cottage. I imagine these occult powers of reflection, refraction, restriction, revision, as crucial to any queer optics if they are to be grounded in practice, ground into the lenses we make all our lives with our bodies and the experiences that shape us. I engrave the word 'QUEER OPTICS' into glass and imagine a queer optics that blots out a lot of queer theory, generating ways of seeing the world with an understanding of where we're standing, and where other people are standing, but also experimenting with distances and angles to play with the possibilities of light and colour. Of course the problem with advocating for a theory that *comes from* practice (like, most recently, Sarah Schulman does in *Let the Record Show*), is that everything has been so hyper-theorized, it's hard to know where to begin. Following *Blue*, beginning with visions, bold colours, shapes, some of the earliest things humans develop to grapple with the world—and contemplating their partiality or loss—feels like as good a place as any.

***

For what are you seeking? The fathomless blue of Bliss. In 2014 Jarman's friend Donald Smith curated a show *Almost Bliss: Notes on Derek Jarman's* Blue, at Chelsea Space, and there the notebook was on display to see your reflection in, to scry with, to capture the power of the stars, to force you into mourning that he was dead. The title page is in Jarman's beautiful handwriting over a painted field of ultramarine blue. A challenge: to get to the fathomless bliss of *Blue*.

When you want something bad enough an archive emerges around it, like in *Almost Bliss*. Or maybe that's just me, researching, researching, researching. I might never, ever get what I want, but you can be sure I'll have a big fucking archive about it, *A Blueprint to Bliss*. Pretty much everything that survives from "history" is a remnant of this kind of desire. My desire in this case, for *Blue* before *Blue*, for *BLISS*, for a mentor I will never meet, calls to assembly: the ultramarine pigment and little shards of lapis lazuli I buy at a crystal shop; there's a script I have that was published in 1993 by Channel 4 Television and BBC Radio 3 "to accompany Blue - a film by Derek Jarman first shown on Channel 4 and simultaneously broadcast on Radio 3 in September 1993" ("First Impression: 3,000 copies," who are my other 2,999 comrades?); a first edition of *Chroma* (1994) in the dust jacket with a portrait of Jarman in a blue-black trench coat holding a coiled, round object in front of his right eye with two outer coils coloured blue, and the inner three coloured red, in the centre his eye (taken by Howard Sooley); a slip of paper advertising *The Blue Concert: A tribute to Derek Jarman*, at the Royal Albert Hall, Saturday 10 June 1995. And on my altar, I keep a light blue glass bottle I bought at an antique shop in Rye before making pilgrimage to Dungeness one bright blue day—it's filled with blue fisherman's twine, driftwood, sea glass, from the beach there.

Instead of sunlight to beam through this assemblage, there is the crushing ambiance/awareness of the infinite prismatic forms (symptoms) refracting the spectrum of experiences of the AIDS crisis, now shot through generations, and continuing to do so. Any meditation on *Blue* begins and ends from that location on earth—*I place a delphinium, blue, upon your grave.* On the level of colour, I'm not so sure, feel there's something more in lapis lazuli, in the ultramarine itself that stays with you even after the movie's over. *Ultramarine,* meaning *beyond the sea,* gesturing toward the 14th-century East-to-West trade networks that brought the pigment from mountains in Afghanistan where the lapis lazuli was mined. *(Why is the sky blue?* If you had ultramarine blue in your illuminated manuscripts or paintings or, say, a fresco by Giotto at the Scrovegni Chapel (c. 1305), *it was because you were wealthy.)* The ultramarine screen brings us into our own particular relationship to blue, but also has the potential to ground us in a completely different reality. Jarman, who cites the writings of Marsilio Ficino—that neo-platonic hermetic homosocial dreamboat—in his diaries and *Chroma,* gives us the lapis lazuli of *Blue* for healing. And maybe even the lapis lazuli for prosperity, for healthcare for all. Ficino wrote that ultramarine should be worn, and worked into architecture to counteract the influence of Saturn—the grim oppressive state, the father who devours his children. Ficino in *Chroma*: "we dedicate the sapphire colour to Jove to whom the sapphire itself is said to be consecrated — that is why lapis lazuli is given its colour — because of its jovial power against black bile. It has a special place among doctors, and it is born with gold, distinct with gold marks." An ultramarine balm to heal, a blue to carry you beyond the sea of your tears.

Brooke Palmieri

EM'S FAVOURITE HART CRANE

EM's favourite hart crane is *twisted by the love of things irreconcilable*. my favourite hart crane is Hart Crane.
What language is that? A poem in a name. He had no chance. The language of blue what is it? Pools of shimmering dada-ist plums and noticings. The frost blue of HIV is what Jarman called

Polyphony.

Flightless

Mannish muff diving disco dick-downiness swan clean the freaking thirst the first of firsts the January first of firsts the patient rush of aeons and sun cuttings strewn for more sun next year! Here's hoping!

If only and

we were so...

wet ready new and young.

D Mortimer

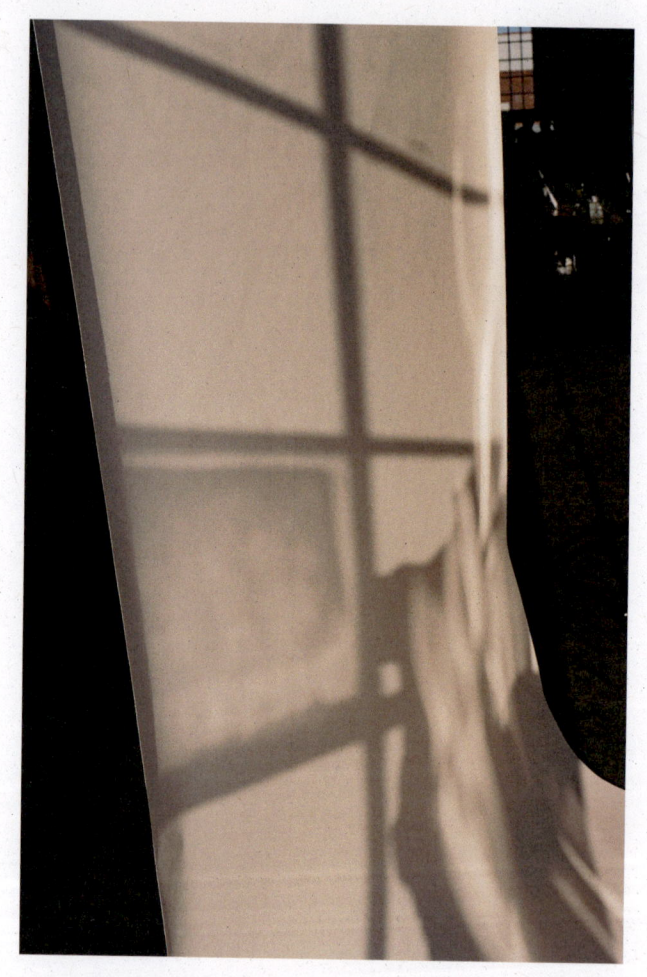

Mary Manning

#0000FF

Saint Jude the Apostle motionless
As the crescent moon hangs low
Crisp white light
Fluorescent bright

OPEN YOUR EYES
Come forth! Arise! Ascend!

Look left
No Blue
Look down
No Blue
Look up
No Blue
Look right
No Blue

Belladonna! Belladonna! Belladonna!
No Italian goddess
Antagonist to restrict eyes to nothing more than

O tomatoes
Look left
O potatoes
Look up
O aubergine
Look right

St Bartholomew's
Frederick Andrewes
An uneasy feeling descends upon me
Christopher Andrewes
I have never ventured inside
Not one of those who forgets history

Invisible and abstract with sixteen tons of pressure
I'm watching this thing move around in my environment
Do you have permission to be here?
I don't remember inviting you
It has no shape

In innocence
They do not know why
Until all the dots are connected
I want to stop the slowly drawn line
Approaching me from the distance

The sound of the man standing on the street trying to scream
I find myself opposite him
Phone in hand
The world has stopped
As I stare at the clock tower

The beating summer sun covering us in a silver waxen glow
Motionless
Hello...
Whispering from the phone
What now
Where should I go?

How will I be perceived?
Nameless?
No
Here I have a name
Aaron

The state of being uncertain will always remain
The needle slamming down
Into a faded blue line
Once a month
I turn my head
And shut my eyes
But feeling fine

I can walk away from this
Nothing attached to me
A pill pot in my pocket
160602
Aaron James Murphy

Saint Raphael the Archangel motionless
The summer sun hugs
The azure skies
Fluorescent bright
Peeling out along the way

ART
What are the limits to the human body?

The most common side effects of SYMTUZA:
Diarrhoea
Rash
Nausea
Fatigue
Headache
Stomach problems
Gas
Severe side effects of SYMTUZA:
Fever
Tiredness
Muscle or joint pain
Blisters or skin lesions
Red or inflamed eyes
Immune system changes
Kidney failure
Diabetes
Lactic acidosis
Increased bleeding

Saint Jude the Apostle   Saint Raphael the Archangel

The more one knows the further one goes
MUSIC!
LIGHTS!
ACTION!

An undetectable viral load is where antiretroviral treatment has reduced the amount of HIV in the body to such small quantities it can no longer be detected by standard blood tests. People living with HIV who have an undetectable viral load cannot pass on HIV through sexual intercourse.

Being undetectable does not mean one has been cured, rather the virus is supressed into smaller amounts. If one were to stop taking the antiroviral treatment the virial load could increase affecting one's health and potentially making the virus transmittable again.

Antiretroviral Treatment also known as Antiretroviral Therapy of ART is a combination of drugs which control HIV. There are lots of combinations and finding the right one is important in keeping the virus under control and the immune system protected.

CD4 count measures the health of the immune system and how advance the virus is. People living with HIV often have a low CD4 count, resulting in a weaker immune system and a vulnerability to infections.

ART stops HIV from multiplying, reduce the levels of HIV and improve CD4 count. With good healthcare and treatment people living with HIV can expect to live a healthy and normal life.

It's no longer a death sentence
throw yourself into life

7:30am alarm buzzes
A gentle reminder
Time to take my art
A combination in one
Darunavir 800mg
Cobicistat 150mg
Emtricitabine 200mg
Tenofovir Alafenamide 10mg
No bitter taste
The size of a suppository
Each time I'm reminded
Of how lucky I am
In control
Supressing
Undetectable
And proud

Look forward

Walking along the beach in a howling gale
Ambition and hope in the rising winter sun
A love which has been found
In the dawns first light
Undetectable and pure
We stand
Lost boys
Embraced
The smell of him so sweet
Good looking
Kiss me
And
Another year happily passes

712213 – 160602
190294 - 000033

Aaron James Murphy

Roelof Bakker

Contributors

In order of appearance

Roelof Bakker
Jared Davis
Becca Albee
Linda Kemp
Ashleigh A. Allen
David Nash
Sam Moore
Anton Stuebner
Gonçalo Lamas
Olivia Laing
Nate Lippens
Jason Lipeles
JP Seabright
Andrew Cummings
Sig Olson
Maria Sledmere
Cleo Henry
Jessie McClaughlin
Lars Meijer
Scott Treleaven
Declan Wiffen
Caitlin Merrett King
Harry Agius
António Manso Preto
Adriana Lazarova
Brooke Palmieri
D Mortimer
Mary Manning
Aaron James Murphy